# WITH SCOTT TO THE POLE

CAPTAIN SCOTT BEFORE HIS FINAL MARCH SOUTH.

# WITH SCOTT TO THE POLE

Re-told by
HOWARD MARSHALL

*Illustrated from the original Photographs*

LONDON
COUNTRY LIFE LIMITED

The passages from Captain Scott's journal are quoted from *Captain Scott's Last Expedition* by kind permission of the publisher, Mr. John Murray.

Photographs by H. G. Ponting, with the exception of the plates facing pages 32 (bottom) and 37 taken by Captain Scott; facing pages 35, 36 and 45 taken by Lieutenant Bowers and that facing page 46 by the Search Party. Taken during the British Antarctic Expedition, 1910–13 (copyright Paul Popper, London).

FIRST PUBLISHED 1936
REPRINTED 1941
REPRINTED 1942

*Made and Printed in Great Britain by*
*Hazell, Watson and Viney Ltd., London and Aylesbury.*

# List of Illustrations

GROTTO IN AN ICEBERG; *TERRA NOVA* IN THE DISTANCE.

"THE LITTLE SHIP LEFT PORT CHALMERS ON THE LAST STAGE OF HER JOURNEY."

# With Scott to the Pole

AT five o'clock on the evening of 1st June, 1910, a little ship cast off her moorings in the South-West India Docks, and nosed out into London River.

Nothing strange about that, perhaps, for ships leave the London docks for the ends of the earth every day of the week. For hundreds of years ships have slipped quietly away on the tide, to sail into adventure or romance. Romance, indeed, is a commonplace on London River.

This little ship, however, spick and span—barque-rigged, her yards square—her hatch covers shining with fresh white paint, trim and workmanlike, was sailing into history. Her name was *Terra Nova*. Already she was scarred by the Antarctic ice, and the sympathetic eye of the expert would have recognised her as an old traveller in dangerous waters. She was bound for her last adventure, the greatest adventure of all. She carried the nucleus of Captain Robert Falcon Scott's expedition to the South Pole.

She was an old Scottish whaler, splendidly strong, and for twenty years she had been working in the Northern pack-ice on whaling and sealing voyages. Just the sort of ship for the expedition, though her coal consumption was high.

Lieut. E. R. Evans collaborated with Scott in the task of fitting her out. He fell in love with her the moment he saw her in the West India Docks. " She looked so small and out of place," he said, " surrounded by great liners and cargo-carrying ships . . . so dirty and uncared for, and yet her name will be remembered for ever in the story of the sea."

She had to be altered and provisioned and stored—no easy matter when we remember where she was sailing, away up into the desolate Polar regions. An ice-house was fitted on the upper deck to hold 150 carcasses of frozen meat; a new stove in the galley; a lamp room, store-

7

rooms, instrument and chronometer rooms, laboratories on the poop and two magazines, all these had to be planned and provided. Above all, every pound had to buy the best possible value.

Still, there it was, the job had to be done; and when at last on 1st June she made her way between the tall liners, Lieut. Evans and his crew had every reason to be satisfied with her. True, there were some anxious moments at Cardiff when, complete with fuel and settling deeply in the water, it was discovered that the seams leaked badly; but, if half an hour's pumping every watch was the worst of the troubles ahead, no one would complain.

Away out of Cardiff to the Breakston Light small craft of every kind accompanied the *Terra Nova*, and on 15th June Lundy Island passed astern and the long swell of the Atlantic lifted the bows of the little ship.

Madeira was the first port of call. At Funchal there was a two days' wait for coaling and magnetic observations; then, once away into the north-east trade winds, the fires were let out and the *Terra Nova* was under sail.

She was heading for New Zealand, where the final preparations for the Expedition were to be made. Then on to be first at the South Pole—no wonder that over eight thousand men had volunteered to make the journey with Scott.

An oddly assorted party they were on board the *Terra Nova*, and the voyage helped them to shake down and get to know one another. Most of them were naval men, but the Expedition also had a wide programme of research, and a number of scientists were accordingly selected. Among these men were Dr. E. A. Wilson, zoologist, in charge of the scientific staff; A. Cherry-Garrard, assistant zoologist; G. C. Simpson, the meteorologist; T. Griffith Taylor, the geologist; E. W. Nelson, the biologist; Charles Wright, the physicist; and also there were the men who had charge of special departments—Cecil Meares, for example, who looked after the dogs, Bernard Day, the motor engineer; the two surgeons, G. Murray Levick and Edward Atkinson; Herbert Ponting, the photographer. Then, among the naval officers, the Army had two representatives: Henry R. Bowers, Lieut., R.I.M., and L. E. G. Oates, Captain in the 6th Inniskilling Dragoons.

This mixed crew settled down splendidly. The scientists trimmed coal, reefed and steered, and everyone took a share in whatever work had to be done, under the leadership of Lieut. Evans.

Captain Scott did not join the ship until it reached Capetown. He was busy doing the one side of the work he disliked—raising money. Before he left England Scott worked hard in the North and in London to raise funds to buy and equip his ship. This quiet, unassuming man was miserable in the rôle of beggar, even in such a heart-stirring cause as this. But after the first £10,000 was raised and this was followed by a Government grant of £20,000, the Expedition funds began to swell. Once aboard the ship in Capetown he began to push ahead with his preparations. There was so much to be done to ensure the success of the Expedition.

A complete programme for work in winter quarters had to be drawn up, and Captain Scott went at it with the thoroughness which characterised everything he undertook. Lieut. Evans noted that " it was an enormous advantage for us to have our leader with us now, his master mind foresaw every situation so wonderfully as he unravelled plan after plan and organised our future procedure."

Ration lists were drawn up: food and thirst were estimated to the spoonful; the seamen were set to overhauling the sledge gear, making fur bags, and perfecting the travelling equipment. The Expedition was taking shape and men were beginning to understand what would be expected of them. From a vaguely imagined adventure, Captain Scott was laying down the foundations of a scientifically organised attack upon the Pole.

In Melbourne, during some of these early preparations, he received a telegram:

" Beg leave inform you proceeding Antarctic—AMUNDSEN."
Seven small words; but momentous words to Captain Scott at the beginning of his adventure.

At Lyttelton in New Zealand the remaining members of the party formed up, among them Meares and Bruce, who had been travelling through Siberia collecting the ponies and sledge dogs—savage animals with much of the wolf in them, but perfectly built for the hard work which lay before them.

Meares put in much hard work choosing these dogs; and giving them driving tests was a responsible business. In one of the trials they turned on a horse and nearly pulled it to pieces before they could be driven off. When he had picked thirty-four dogs and twenty good ponies, Meares had to arrange their transport, by an endless succession of trains and steamers, through a wearying series of inoculations and disinfectings, before their goal was reached—the *Terra Nova* in New Zealand. Although the dogs had suffered from the heat, there were no losses—a great credit to Meares' patience and care.

So six months passed, and on 29th November, 1910, the little ship left Port Chalmers on the last stage of her journey. At last the Expedition was really together, headed for the unknown; and the *Terra Nova* was a happy ship, but a queer, overcrowded one. The upper deck looked like a miniature zoo, with the dogs chained to stanchions and ring bolts, and white ponies looking out of their stalls.

The *Terra Nova*, indeed, was crammed with the essential stores and equipment. Sacks of coal were wedged among the deck cargo; paraffin and oil drums filled up the hatch spaces; more than forty-five tons of fodder for the ponies and five tons of dog biscuits had to be squeezed in somewhere; and then there was a miscellaneous collection of gear to be stored away, such as carpenters' stores, blacksmith's outfit, lubricating oils, fireworks for signalling and so on.

With the ship so deeply laden, weather conditions were important, and it was a serious matter when she ran into a tearing gale. Lieut. Evans hove her to; but huge waves broke over the decks, and the wretched dogs were almost strangled in their chains.

First one pony died—then another. Oates watched over them constantly, himself drenched and bitterly cold, but only concerned for the animals under his charge. No one who saw Oates struggling to help the wretched ponies would ever forget him: there he stood, in the meagre light of a hanging lamp, seeming at moments to be lifting the ponies to their feet by a superhuman effort, as heavy seas washed their legs from under them.

The coarse coal bags were picked up and washed against the lashed crates, which broke loose; for hours all hands strove in the hold of the

CAPTAIN OATES WITH PONIES AND DOGS AT SEA.

"THE SHIP HEAVED AND STRAINED AND PITCHED LIKE A CORK."

ship, trying to make everything fast, heaving the coal sacks overboard, submerged now and again by the mountainous seas which swept the decks continuously.

Night fell; sea and wind rose; the ship heaved and strained and pitched like a cork. The men laboured unceasingly. Oates and Atkinson stayed with the ponies, trying to keep them on their legs, and at 4 a.m. Captain Scott received a report from the engine room that the pumps had choked.

This was serious indeed. The water gained; the decks were leaking; the ship might become waterlogged; the chief engineer had to draw his fires. On deck the scenes were terrible. The dogs choked; the ponies floundered in the swirling water; the lee bulwarks were torn away, and the sea washed over endlessly.

There were moments when Captain Scott and Lieut. Evans despaired. Terrible to think that the *Terra Nova* might founder in this black horror of wind and gale and darkness: and yet the prospect was cheerless indeed. Fortunately the seamen were the pick of the Navy and the Mercantile Marine, and they worked magnificently.

Evans organised the afterguard in two parties to bale with buckets, and, although the attempt seemed almost pathetically futile, it actually succeeded in keeping the water under. For a night and a day this baling continued. From Captain Scott downwards, all took their turn, wading often waist deep in the water, covered with oil and coal dust, passing the buckets up, torn and racked with weariness.

Meanwhile Williams, the engineer, was toiling in the heat behind the boiler, cutting a hole in the engine room bulkhead to get at the suction of the pump. A dog was drowned, a pony died, another dog was washed overboard by one wave and swept back by the next. The baling went on; the hole in the bulkhead was cut, Lieut. Evans wriggled over the coals and managed to make his way down the shaft. There, sitting on the keel, with water up to his neck, he remained for two hours, clearing the obstruction in the pump. Often he had to plunge into the filthy water, and he sent up twenty buckets full of oil and coal dust.

Though the bilges had been washed out in New Zealand, a good deal of coal dust had since found its way into them. A mixture of this dust and lubricating oil, which had washed down from the engines, had formed lumps—the cause of the trouble. Lieut. Evans had to go head first under the foul water and it was days before he and his helpers got really clean again.

Gradually the pumps began to gain, and slowly the gale subsided. The danger was past, and the *Terra Nova* steamed south once more within two points of her course.

Wilson, in his journal, described a curious incident which impressed him about this affair. " . . . Just about the time when things looked their very worst—the sky was like ink and water was everywhere and everyone was as wet inside their oilskins as the skins were wet without—there came out a most perfect and brilliant rainbow for about half a minute or less and then suddenly and completely went out. If ever there was a moment when such a message was a comfort it was just then; it seemed to remove every shadow of doubt not only as to the present, but as to the final issue of the whole expedition. And from that moment matters mended, and everything came all right."

Throughout this grim experience the members of the party had kept their spirits up splendidly. Captain Scott tells us that they sang chanties as they worked: a good omen for the arduous days to come.

In consequence of the gale the main deck under the forecastle leaked badly and the dirt of the stable trickled through on to the men's hammocks and bedding. Those who had quarters in that part did the best they could to protect their bedding with canvas and oilskins; not a word was said, but Scott knew and appreciated his men's determination that there should be no grumbling.

On Wednesday, 7th December, they sighted their first iceberg. Soon the *Terra Nova* was passing close beside all kinds of bergs and Lieut. Evans described them as " like great masses of sugar floating in the sea." Whalebirds, sooty albatrosses and mollymawks were presently joined by brown-backed petrels—a sure sign that the pack ice was not far away. Now the *Terra Nova* was butting through the treacherous stuff—heavy, hummocked bay ice with floes seven and eight feet out of the water—a severe strain on the ship. Captain Scott wondered whether he had done wisely to come so far east. On 13th December they were fast imprisoned.

Fortunately open water returned, but for 400 miles they had to make this laborious progress, working slowly through the frozen sea, stopping sometimes for days, with fires out and sails furled, but doggedly pushing on whenever the chance came. A wearisome, irritating business for men anxious to press ahead with the real work of the expedition; but still they remained cheerful, making their observations, exercising on skis, peering from the crow's-nest for a way through; watching the sea leopards and Emperor penguins and the great whales; taking photographs and celebrating Christmas Day, when Captain Scott wrote in his diary:

" The scene is altogether too Christmassy. Ice surrounds us, low nimbus clouds intermittently discharging light snowflakes obscure the sky, here and there small pools of open water throw shafts of black shadow on to the cloud—this black predominates in the direction from which we have come, elsewhere the white haze of ice blink is pervading.

" We are captured. We do practically nothing under sail to push through, and could do little under steam, and at each step forward the possibility of advance seems to lessen."

To Wilson, as an artist, there were compensations, which must have been shared to some degree by the others. He was enchanted with the broad daylight, night and day, " the beauty of the day with its lovely blues and greens amongst the bergs and ice floes—eclipsed altogether by the marvellous beauty of the midnight, when white ice becomes deepest purple and golden rose and the sky is lemon green without a cloud. No scene in the whole world," he wrote in his journal, " was ever more beautiful than a clear midnight in the pack."

But, for all that, these were tantalising conditions; still the party was happy. Crean's rabbit produced a family, and the crew had a very merry evening, with a dinner of tomato soup, stewed penguin breast, roast beef, plum pudding, mince pies, asparagus, champagne, port and liqueurs.

This was merely an interlude, though, and for twenty days the pack held them. They used sixty-one tons of coal in forcing their way through, at the rate of eighteen miles a day, and only six miles to the ton. Even so, Captain Scott could write: " The spirit of the enterprise is as bright as ever. Every one strives to help every one else, and not a word of complaint or anger has been heard on board."

13

The penguins gave some light relief. Singing attracted them quickly, and a penguin audience might often be seen listening to a group of explorers on the poop singing in raucous voices: " For she's got bells on her fingers and rings on her toes, elephants to ride upon wherever she goes." Meares was the favourite turn: his rendering of " God Save the King " generally sent the listeners to the water.

It was not until the last day of 1910 that patience was rewarded. They had reached the Ross Sea, and a south-westerly gale had been blowing. Gradually the squalls lessened, and at 10 p.m. the clouds lifted.

Captain Scott looked towards the west and saw the great mountains lying in the sunshine. Mount Sabine stood out sharply, although it was 110 miles away, so marvellously clear was the antarctic atmosphere.

Here for the first time Man saw an Emperor penguin chick still in the down stage—a period of its life history which had been surmised by naturalists but never actually seen. The young Emperor stood beside its sleeping parent on a piece of old ice about ten feet square, now pressed up six feet above the water-level.

This was the beginning of the real adventure. If thoughts of Amundsen's telegram occurred, they were not allowed to distract Scott from his chosen course. Actually Amundsen in the *Fram* was sixty miles to the north, but the sense of rivalry was not yet acute. There were more immediate problems—where to land the most pressing of them. Scott and Nelson were anxious to have the beach at Cape Crozier as their base: it would mean a shorter journey to the Pole.

The *Terra Nova* sighted the Cape on 3rd January, and Evans took her in close to the face of the Great Ice Barrier. Captain Scott went off in a whale boat to look for a landing-place, but found a heavy swell running under the rich brown and yellow cliffs. A strange sight they must have been, those Crozier cliffs, with their twisted columns of basalt, and the hanging icicles everywhere; a strange sight from the whale boat riding the long swell. Disappointing also, for landing was out of the question, and the *Terra Nova* set course for McMurdo Sound.

The party had a narrow shave at this time. While they were rowing along under the overhanging Crozier cliffs someone jokingly remarked

14

THE APPROACH TO THE PACK-ICE.

"FOR TWENTY DAYS THE PACK HELD THEM."

"THEY SIGHTED THEIR FIRST ICEBERG."

that it would be a " short-lived amusement " to see the cliff above break away and fall over on them.   When the boat was some 200 yards on its way back to the ship, there was a deafening noise, a great fall into the sea and a cloud of rock dust.   That very thing had happened—the "joke" had all but come off.

Round Cape Bird they went, and Captain Scott picked up the old landmarks—Mount Discovery and the Western Mountains.   The familiar sight encouraged him: the disappointment of Cape Crozier became less acute.   Perhaps it would be better on this side of the island. He watched killer whales catching penguins, and noted with satisfaction the progress of the ship through the pack ice near the shore.

They sailed past Cape Royds, unexpectedly in clear water; past Cape Barne and Inaccessible Island, and so to an excellent beach which they used to call the Skuary, where the conditions would be perfect.   As they steered for the fast ice the ship's stern struck, and they made fast with ice anchors.   They had a solid wharf where they could land their stores, and a road to the Cape.   This was a better ending to their journey than had seemed possible.   Captain Scott was greatly encouraged.   The first stage of the adventure was over.   The luck had turned.

The landing at Cape Evans was followed by a week's intensive work. The stores had to be discharged, the motor sledges were unpacked, the ponies were picketed on the floe, the hut was erected, the provisions were stored.   With remarkable speed the long level beach began to look, as Captain Scott contentedly remarked, like an orderly camp.

There were misadventures of course.   Several people, Atkinson and Bruce among them, suffered from snow blindness; sore faces and lips and blistered feet were common.   Ponting had the most unpleasant adventure.   Out one morning alone, with his sledge laden with cameras and cinematograph, his glasses misty with perspiration, he suddenly felt the ice giving way under him.   There was no one near to whom he could shout for help.   He lunged forward, the ice yielding ominously beneath his feet, the sledge lurching through the water.   Fortunately the bad patch was not extensive and he pulled out on to a firm surface, none the worse.   But this incident served to show Scott the perils of such decaying ice.   He said at this time: " The elements are going to be troublesome,

15

but it is good to know them as the only adversary and to feel there is so small a chance of internal friction."

Then came a disastrous day—8th January—when the third motor sledge went through the sludgy ice. Campbell tried to rush it across a weak patch, and suddenly it disappeared, with the rope, by which the men held it, cutting through the ice towards them. This was one of the two best motors, and to lose it in so unexpected a way was a great disappointment to Scott.

In six days the expedition was landed, not without incident. One morning Scott saw about six killer whales astern of the *Terra Nova*, their snouts well out of the water. The two Esquimaux dogs were tethered close by the water's edge to the wire stern rope of the ship. Ponting rushed towards the floe edge with his camera to photograph the whales, which for the moment had disappeared. Immediately the floe beneath him and the dogs was heaved up, the ice rocking dangerously as the whales hit it with their backs from underneath. By great good fortune Ponting kept his balance and was able to dash to safety; neither of the dogs fell through the splits in the ice and obviously the whole thing was a great surprise to the whales. They rose up through the clefts they had made to see what was happening—an awful sight with " their small glistening eyes, and their terrible array of teeth—by far the largest and most terrifying in the world." One of the whales must have been within five feet of a dog.

It was a revelation to Scott, he wrote, that these creatures could break up ice at least two and a half feet thick, " and that they could act in unison . . . it is clear that they are endowed with singular intelligence and in future we shall treat that intelligence with every respect."

However, despite minor alarms like this, Scott was pleased. " Nothing like it has been done before; nothing so expeditious and complete," was his verdict. A good omen; and the party was in correspondingly high spirits.

The landing-place was christened Hurrah Beach, and the bay to the northward of the winter quarters Happy Bay. Then everyone settled down to prepare for the first depot-laying journey. They were getting ready the road to the Pole, laying down their stores of provisions along

"THE LANDING AT THE ICE-FOOT NEAR CAPE EVANS."

"THE MOTOR SLEDGES WERE UNPACKED AND LANDED."

"THE HUT WAS ERECTED."

the route. For most of the party this experience of antarctic journeying was new, and strange and interesting indeed they must have found it. Even Scott, familiar with the conditions, was moved to record impressions which bring the scene before us vividly.

In his diary he noted: " The seductive folds of the sleeping-bag. The hiss of the primus and the fragrant steam of the cooker issuing from the tent ventilator. The small green tent and the great white road. The whine of a dog and the neigh of our steeds. The driving cloud of powdered snow. The crunch of footsteps which break the surface crust. The wind-blown furrows. The blue arch beneath the smoky cloud. The crisp ring of the ponies' hoofs and the swish of the following sledge. The droning conversation of the march as driver encourages or chides his horse. The patter of dog pads. The gentle flutter of our canvas shelter. Its deep booming sound under the full force of a blizzard. The drift snow like finest flour penetrating every hole and corner— flickering up beneath one's head covering, pricking sharply as a sand blast. The sun with blurred image peeping shyly through the wreathing drift giving pale shadowless light. The eternal silence of the great white desert. Cloudy columns of snowdrift advancing from the south, pale yellow wraiths, heralding the coming storm, blotting out one by one the sharp-cut lines of the land. The blizzard, Nature's protest—the crevasse, Nature's pitfall—that grim trap for the unwary—no hunter could conceal his snare so perfectly—the light rippled snow bridge gives no hint or sign of the hidden danger, its position unguessable till man or beast is floundering, clawing and struggling for foothold on the brink. The vast silence broken only by the mellow sounds of the marching column."

There is the picture—that vast silence, that great white road, the powdered snow dancing across the blue arch of the sky, the sounds which pointed the silence—crunch of feet, ring of ponies' hoofs, murmur of voices—and at the end of the day the small green tent, a green speck in the waste of snow—green upon the endless white—green blades thrusting through the ice furrows—the uprising of man's will to conquer.

So they went in that pale shadowless light—twelve men, eight ponies, thirty-six dogs—small moving specks across the snow, working to a plan. At nine in the morning they would turn out of their sleeping-bags—

the temperature outside five or six degrees below zero—and Scott would shout to Oates: " How are things? " Then bitterly cold work harnessing the ponies and leading the sledge, and taking the ponies to the sledges. Odd jobs to be done, while those who were ready waited impatiently with numbed fingers on their horses' bridles, feeling the biting wind from which even the ponies turned their heads away. At last the party would be all set, and Scott would say, " All right, Bowers, go ahead."

Then the column settled down to marching; now and again someone slipped and fell on the icy surface; the light was dim and grey; the going hard. There would be a halt half-way through the day—tents up, cooker going, ponies covered; and then on again through the twilit silence until eight o'clock, when the last camp was made, and snow walls built for the animals.

Scott was distressed now because of the ponies' difficulty in making headway over patches of soft snow. One would flounder and plunge, jerk the sledge frantically behind it and land on a firm surface exhausted with the strain. The only thing was to let a sure-footed pony pick a way and keep the others back until the best route was found.

" What extraordinary uncertainties this work exhibits! " wrote Scott of these complications. " Every day some new fact comes to light—some new obstacle which threatens the greatest obstruction. I suppose this is the reason which makes the game so well worth playing."

This depot-laying journey was valuable in many ways. It accustomed the men to the conditions, and gave Scott much information about the capacities of the dogs and ponies.

The dogs, he noted, were getting a little fierce. Two white dogs, which had been trained to go for strangers, now began to bark viciously at the approach of anyone but their own driver. One nipped Scott's leg; he had no stick and, had Meares not been on the sledge, the rest of the team would have followed the lead and been at Scott in a moment.

But this journey nearly saw a much more serious disaster, for on the return Scott and Wilson missed falling into a sixty-five feet deep crevasse by inches. Their dog team went over the edge, and hung dangling on the harness in the abyss, swaying and howling and snarling; two dogs fell to the bottom. Scott, Wilson and Meares worked desperately to rescue

LEFT BEHIND IN VICTORIA LAND.

THE PARTY GOES INTO WINTER QUARTERS.

THE RAMPARTS OF MT. EREBUS.

them, and at last Scott was lowered on an Alpine rope to send up the last two animals.

The seals were another trial—they were very troublesome to Meares and Wilson with their dogs. The teams went mad when they saw them. Wilson wrote in his journal: " Occasionally when one pictures oneself quite away from trouble of that kind, an old seal will pop his head up at a blowhole a few yards ahead of the team, and they are all on top of him before one can say ' Knife '! Then one has to rush in with the whip— and every one of the team of eleven jumps over the harness of the dog next to him and the harnesses become a muddle that takes much patience to unravel, not to mention care lest the whole team should get away with the sledge and its load and leave one behind to follow on foot at leisure. . . . Several times I had only time to seize a strap or a part of the sledge and be dragged along helter-skelter over everything that came in the way till the team got sick of galloping and one could struggle to one's feet again."

But all the same the drivers got very attached to their dogs. Wilson was fond of his leader, " who looks in face as if he knew all the wickedness of all the world and all its cares and as if he were bored to death by them."

Then there was trouble with a pony. The party had done six and a half miles of the day's march one day when the vanguard noticed that Weary Willy had dropped about three-quarters of a mile behind. The dog teams were getting near and suddenly there was a sound of distant barking. Oates and Scott turned back, guessing something had gone wrong. They met Meares, who reported that his dog team had got out of control and had attacked the pony when it fell. Gran broke his ski stick and Meares his dog stick trying to beat them off, and the pony himself made a gallant fight, shaking some of the dogs in his teeth. Scott thought this accident taught them more about the surface than hours of pony leading: for four of the party had to go back and drag up Weary Willy's load. Characteristically the leader blamed himself for not supervising matters better and noticing that Willy was more heavily loaded than the other ponies.

On Wednesday, 22nd February, came a much worse shock which

19

plainly worried Scott, though he does not give it undue prominence in his diary. When he returned with Wilson, Meares, Evans and Cherry-Garrard to Hut Point, he found a letter from Campbell—left in charge of *Terra Nova*—and Campbell reported a meeting with Amundsen in the Bay of Whales.

Amundsen and his Norwegians—a hard lot of men, said Campbell—were unloading their stores near the Barrier Edge. What is more, Amundsen had landed 120 dogs safely, and with his expert ski-runners he was sixty miles nearer the Pole. It would, moreover, be possible to start early in the season with dogs, another factor in Amundsen's favour.

His plan, in short, was a serious menace to the British Expedition, and Scott recognised it. He wrote at the time: " One thing only fixes itself definitely in my mind. The proper, as well as the wiser, course for us is to proceed exactly as though this had not happened. To go forward and do our best for the honour of the country without fear or panic."

The fact remains that the race was clearly on, and though Scott minimised it and tried to cheer up his companions, they were momentarily depressed by the news. It would be Amundsen's dogs against Scott's ponies, and obviously Scott would have to hasten his dash for the Pole as soon as sledging became practicable after the winter.

In the meantime there was work to do, and Scott very sensibly set his party to it, though still they could not shake off the misfortune which seemed to mark them down.

Fast continuing their preparations for the spring, they ran into blizzards and lost two ponies; and then came an incident which might well have wrecked the Expedition entirely.

As Oates, Gran and Scott approached one of the storage depots, they noticed in the lowering sky mirage effects of huge, broken ice floes. At first Scott thought that this was an optical illusion; but when they came to the depot and found the sea full of broken Barrier ice, Scott was filled with anxiety.

He had sent Bowers, Cherry-Garrard and Crean across the sea ice to Hut Point with four ponies, and now the ice was definitely on the move. Bowers and his party had found the ponies fixed, and their progress was

SLEDGE AND DOGS, WITH MT. EREBUS IN BACKGROUND.

"ON ALL SIDES KILLER WHALES."

slow. As they advanced towards Hut Point, Bowers noticed cracks in the ice, and felt a swell which told him what was happening. He turned his party, and made for land, with the ponies jumping over the increasing cracks, until at last an apparently safe place was found for the night. Camp was pitched, but at 4.30 next morning, when Bowers opened his tent, he found to his horror that they were surrounded by water, and that one of the ponies had fallen into the sea; a terrible situation.

The party struggled desperately until Crean volunteered to go for help. He had a difficult task before him. The sea between the ice floes was seething and furious; on all sides killer whales were putting up their heads, hurling themselves up through the water and trying to get at the ponies.

Bowers and Cherry-Garrard were marooned there with the animals and sledge while Crean went off on his desperate venture. He had to jump from floe to floe towards the Barrier face, and Bowers watched him most anxiously through the telescope in his theodolite. Crean kept steadily on, and managed at last to leap to an ice floe which was swinging towards the face of the Barrier. By great good fortune it touched; Crean was able to spring, take hold and begin to climb the Barrier, with ski-sticks to help him. Bowers was immensely relieved: he knew then that Crean would bring help—possibly a boat from Cape Evans.

Crean, exhausted, did find Scott, and at once the salvage work began. It was not easy, though luckily the ice had stopped drifting, and lay quiet, close to the Barrier Edge.

They were able to get the men and sledges ashore, but as they lifted the last loads they saw that the ice was beginning to drift again, and the ponies had to be left till the morning. The exhausted rescue party turned in, worn out by exertion, worry and lack of sleep. In the morning it was found that the ponies had drifted away. Bowers saw them a mile to the north-west. Again the work of rescue began. It was decided to rush the ponies across the ice. Two fell in and had to be destroyed— these incidents, said Scott, were too terrible—but the remaining beast was saved.

A tragic affair, and the loss of the three ponies was serious. Mercifully, though, Bowers, Crean and Cherry-Garrard had come through safely, and the sledge and equipment had been salvaged. If all had gone Scott's plans would have been thrown out entirely, and the future of the expedition jeopardised.

This was a narrow escape, but then such perils were inevitable, and Scott accepted them with remarkable patience. Always he looked ahead. Once danger had passed he put it aside completely and busied his active mind with the next task.

He was anxious to return to headquarters at Cape Evans, but he had to wait until the sea ice formed safely again over the fifteen miles of water between them. The party settled down patiently at Discovery Hut, thawing out some old newspapers which had been left there by a previous expedition, improving the hut, making blubber lamps and taking what exercise they could. Meanwhile the sea was watched anxiously for signs of freezing. The weather was unkind, with continuous wind rising sometimes to gale force, and now and again unexpected warmth which melted the ice on the inner roof of the hut and sent streams of water down the walls.

The party numbered sixteen, and fortunately they were men of widely varying experiences. Between them they had travelled in every country in the world, and they could pass the time in exercise and reminiscent gossiping.

Competition amongst the cooks was keen and there was much rivalry. Supper with an invariable basis of fried seal liver would not seem to offer much variety. But Scott remarks that " a lot can be done with a little flour, a handful of raisins, a spoonful of curry powder, or the addition of a little boiled pea meal." Wilson nearly spoiled his reputation as a culinary genius by experimenting with penguin blubber for frying the liver. His efforts reduced all but three stalwarts to a supper of cocoa and biscuits.

It was fortunate that everyone managed to sleep eight or nine hours without interruption; and by the light of blubber lamps and candles it was possible to read for an hour or so.

It was a wearing, trying time, though, despite the comfort they achieved, and even Scott's monumental patience showed signs of wear. For six weeks they were held prisoners. Winter was approaching. The

"SCOTT WROTE AND PLANNED AND CALCULATED AT HIS LITTLE TABLE."

"TO WILSON, AS AN ARTIST, THERE WERE COMPENSATIONS."

CAPTAIN SCOTT'S BIRTHDAY PARTY.

dark shadows added their depressing effects, and the surroundings were sullen and forbidding. Only the indefatigable Wilson managed to extract much profit from this dreary delay, for with numbed fingers he sketched the sinister scene in every varying degree of light and weather.

The conditions, in fact, were very like those which Scott was to meet on his return from the Pole—the tearing wind, the sepulchral light, the heavy snow surface, the temperature which dropped to forty degrees below zero; and if it was depressing then, how much worse it would be for the little party of dispirited, worn and hungry men!

At last, however, on 13th April, the sea ice froze and Scott was able to return to his headquarters for the winter. He was pleased with the hut, delighted with his men. Not only did he admire them for their individual qualities, but he wrote:

" I am very much impressed with the extraordinary and general cordiality of the relations which exist among our people.

" I do not suppose that a statement of the real truth, namely, that there is no friction at all, will be credited—it is so generally thought that the many rubs of such a life as this are quietly and purposely sunk in oblivion. With me there is no need to draw a veil; there is nothing to cover. There are no strained relations in this hut, and nothing more emphatically evident than the universally amicable spirit which is shown on all occasions. . . . It is a triumph to have collected such men."

In a letter home, Scott revealed something of the devotion of his companions. He remarked that it would be a good thing if the officers had some knowledge of navigation, so that in an emergency they would know how to steer a sledge home. " It appears," wrote Scott, " that ' Cherry ' thereupon commenced a serious and arduous course of study of abstruse navigational problems which he found exceedingly tough and now despaired mastering. Of course there is not one chance in a hundred that he will ever have to consider navigation on our journey . . . but it makes matters much easier for me to have men who take the details of one's work so seriously and who strive so simply and honestly to make it successful."

So they settled down happily to face the long winter, and very well they spent it. There was always work going on in the hut. The meteorologists and biologists were collecting and tabulating their dates; there were records kept of wind force and direction, atmospheric electricity, barometric pressure, temperatures.

Wright pushed forward the study of ice physics; Nelson studied the tides and collected drifting organisms from the sea. Cherry-Garrard produced the *South Polar Times*; Oates and Anton, the little Russian, lavished their care on the horses; Meares looked after the dogs.

At one end of the hut, Captain Scott, Wilson and Lieut. Evans worked. Scott wrote and planned and calculated at his little table, covered with green linoleum, with gloves and socks and fur boots hanging on the walls round him, his boots on shelves, a small Union Jack stuck in his pipe-rack, and his old uniform coat covering his bed. (Scott had a sentimental attachment for his twenty-three-year-old coat. It had been " spared neither rain, wind nor salt sea spray, tropic heat nor arctic cold; it has outlived many sets of buttons, from their glittering gilded youth to green old age, and it supports its four-stripe shoulder-straps as gaily as the single lace ring of the early days which proclaimed it the possession of a humble sub-lieutenant.")

This part of the hut was known as Grosvenor Street: " Although hung around with fur mitts, fur boots, socks, hats and woollen clothing, there was something very chaste about this very respectable corner," wrote Evans. " Peeping from under his (Scott's) sleeping-place one could espy an emblem of civilisation and prosperity in the shape of a very good suit-case! "

The hut had been well and truly built, and it was a comfortable and snug house, complete with its bunks and sitting-room, its scientific laboratories and its dark-room, where Ponting worked at the invaluable photographs of the expedition.

Nelson and Day, both tidy people, shared a cubicle and utilised their space amazingly. The biologist's microscope occupied a bench, in the midst of a neat array of enamel dishes and tidily stacked books; there were " two neat bunks with neat, closely curtained drawers for clothing and neat reflecting sconces for candles; overhead was a neat arrangement for drying socks, with several nets, neatly bestowed. The carpentering to produce this effect had been of quite a high order."

24

It was Day who had made the most efficient arrangements for the lighting, heating and ventilating of the hut. But it was Clissold, the guardian of the cooking stove, who was responsible for the hut's most ingenious device. This was a contrivance which arranged that the " rising " of the bread in the oven completed an electric circuit, thus ringing a bell and turning on a red lamp! This gadget was afterwards elaborated and Scott realised that the Expedition had " a very exceptional cook! "

Swiftly the winter closed in on Scott and his men. The cold grew intense, the little daylight diminished until only grey shadows remained; the sky was black above, and the snow a paler shade of grey beneath. It was a world of darkness and desolation, except when the auroral light spread across the sky, a tremulous, iridescent veil of delicate colours, transforming the steely shadows into a spectacle of supreme beauty. This wonderful phenomenon appeared after the party had celebrated mid-winter day with a grand meal of seal soup and roast beef, plum pudding and mince pies.

An odd contrast, this hearty feasting, and the moment when, at the end of it all, Captain Scott looked towards the eastern sky, and saw those luminous streamers of colour, rising wave upon wave, suggesting to the lonely onlookers " something wholly spiritual, something instinct with a fluttering ethereal life."

The days went by busily enough, and the party kept their spirits up splendidly, for they were held together and stimulated by their common objective—the dash for the Pole which would follow when the spring came and the sledges could go out.

Some of them exercised on ski, others led the ponies, and sometimes they played football on the sea ice—a dangerous proceeding. Three times a week they had lectures; most members of the expedition had their special branch of knowledge and could contribute.

Lieut. Evans described " coast lining " as the most interesting work done at this time. This was a branch of surveying. It meant " walking along the edge of the sea ice, fixing one's position by sextant angle every five hundred yards or so, and sketching in a notebook the character and features of the ever-changing coast . . . it meant following carefully round cape and glacier edge, penetrating inlets and delineating every islet, promontory, cliff and talus." And this in a biting wind, with numbed fingers and the constant fear of frost-bite.

Scott was amused during these days to see the way those in charge of the various stores zealously conserved things for " a rainy day." Thus, a storekeeper would closely question an applicant for a piece of canvas; eventually he would admit that there might be a small piece somewhere. In reality several rolls of the material were safely in his keeping.

On the whole life was uneventful, though the perils of the situation were brought home sharply to Scott on 4th July. A blizzard was blowing—the wind between 40 and 45 m.p.h. and the temperature some twenty-eight degrees below zero. No weather to be in the open, as Captain Scott remarked; but in the afternoon the wind dropped slightly, and Atkinson and Gran set out over the floe to look at the North and South Bay thermometers. Gran returned at 6.45, and for a while no one noticed that Atkinson was missing. Then Captain Scott became uneasy. He knew that the atmosphere was very thick, and snow was falling. A paraffin flare was lit on Wind Vane Hill and Petty-Officer Evans took out a search party with lanterns, but returned at 9.30 without news.

By this time Scott was seriously alarmed, particularly when he discovered that Atkinson was wearing only comparatively light clothing. Search parties were promptly organised and despatched with sledges, sleeping-bags and brandy.

Scott was left alone in the hut with Clissold, and his fears for Atkinson's safety increased hourly. Atkinson had only intended to travel a mile from the hut, but he had been missing for five hours. Another hour went by, and then, to Scott's intense relief, Meares and Debenham returned, bringing with them a badly frost-bitten Atkinson.

His story was confused but significant. After making a quarter of a mile he decided to turn back, and very soon lost his sense of direction in the wind and darkness. He stumbled on a fish-trap hole, which he recognised, but, his mind blurred and his reasoning powers weakened by the effects of the blizzard, he took the wrong direction from the hole.

26

VIDA, ONE OF THE DOGS.

NGUIN AND YOUNG.

A BROODING PENGUIN SNOWED IN AFTER BLIZZARD.

What happened to him next Atkinson did not remember. He could not see a yard before him; he wandered aimlessly, tried to put on a frozen fur glove, and had his hand frost-bitten; then he fell into the tide crack, began to dig a hole where he could shelter until rescue arrived, had a glimpse of the moon and wandered out again, steered a better course, saw the flare, and so found his way to safety.

Another narrow escape, and one which showed how dangerous the antarctic weather could be, how numbing to brain as well as limbs the force and cold of a swirling blizzard. Scott welcomed the incident for the practical lesson it gave to his party, and the warning it provided.

About this time Dr. Wilson, Bowers and Cherry-Garrard set out on a winter journey to observe the incubation of the Emperor penguins at their rookery near Cape Crozier. This involved a journey of seventy miles past the Point and the Barrier, with each man pulling a load of 253 lb.—a heavy weight. It was a hazardous undertaking, and the party encountered some of the hardest weather conditions conceivable. The wonder is that they survived, and their feat is one of the most remarkable in antarctic history.

They were away five weeks. When they returned, their faces, says Scott, " were scarred and wrinkled, their eyes dull, their hands whitened and creased with the constant exposure to damp and cold," and they were almost encased in ice.

They had suffered most from lack of sleep. Wilson was very thin, Cherry-Garrard rather worn; Bowers came through best. In Scott's opinion he was " the hardest traveller that ever undertook a Polar journey, as well as one of the most undaunted . . . never was such a sturdy, active, undefeatable little man."

These men had only a thin canvas tent to protect them, and the temperature dropped to —77 degrees, or 109 degrees of frost—conditions which no civilised men had ever before encountered. Blizzard followed blizzard, and they groped onwards in almost complete darkness. Eventually, by sheer determination, a point was reached 800 feet above Cape Crozier. The party built a hut, made their observations with the utmost difficulty, and then were beset by a blizzard which raged for nearly two days. The roof of the hut was blown away; the tent was torn into the darkness; the snow swept down and the men could only huddle in their sleeping-bags, with the snow driving into every fold, every chink and crevice. Meanwhile the wind, as Cherry-Garrard said, was " roaring above them like an express train in a tunnel."

For thirty hours they lay there, frozen and without food. At last the wind relaxed; the tent was discovered a quarter of a mile away, and the homeward journey began.

Again a blizzard struck the party. For two more days they were trapped. Their sleeping-bags were frozen so stiff that the skins split when they tried to bend them; and when an attempt was made to thaw out ice-covered socks and mitts, by putting them in breast pockets at night, it failed entirely.

Bowers's reindeer sleeping-bag weighed 17 lb. before the journey; afterwards the ice it collected brought the weight up to 33 lb. The double tent increased in the same way from 35 lb. to 60 lb.

The cold was incredible, and the misery they suffered stupendous; but they stuck it out, and struggled back to Cape Evans after five weeks in the black heart of the Polar night, battered by terrible gales. A tale of extraordinary courage and strength of purpose which seemed to augur well for the journey to the Pole; and, despite the fantastic hardships, the objects of this winter journey were fulfilled.

Scott was not only proud of his men's courage: he was pleased with the material results. Something was now known of the conditions on the Great Barrier in winter; and some valuable observations on endurance, rations and sleeping-equipment had been made. A sledging ration suitable for the Summit party was evolved from this experience. It consisted of 16 oz. biscuit, 12 oz. pemmican, 3 oz. sugar, 2 oz. butter, 0.7 oz. tea and 0.6 oz. cocoa. The pemmican was made of beef extract with 60 per cent. pure fat: it formed the basis for a thick and nourishing soup. Incidentally, it is interesting to know that the candles specially prepared for Scott's Expedition were edible.

Slowly the winter passed, and on 26th August the return of the sun was celebrated with champagne, and even poems. The ponies frisked with joy, the snow slopes shone with colour—pink, purple, orange—the

DR. WILSON, LIEUT. BOWERS AND CHERRY-GARRARD LEAVING FOR CAPE CROZIER.

ICE BASTIONS OF THE CASTLE BERG.

dogs stretched and wagged their tails; the final stage of the adventure was approaching.

So far everything had gone to plan: the voyage out; the depot-laying journey; the winter of preparation and scientific research; now came the planning of the spring travelling and the final dash to the Pole.

As the Expedition approached its climax, so the spirits of the men increased. Scott and Bowers worked away at the vitally important sledging figures, and here accuracy was essential. They did not know how far the motor sledges would help them, and they had to reckon with the failure of the motors, and leave themselves with an exact margin of safety.

Scott tried to envisage every possible misfortune, and after a week's concentration on detail he felt decidedly optimistic. The animals were in good trim, and Oates gave them plenty of exercise. Meares took the dogs to Corner Camp, and covered sixty miles in two days—fast travelling. Only the weather was unpropitious and occasionally the training of the ponies was held up. Clissold was badly hurt by a fall when climbing: Forde's hand was frost-bitten and Debenham developed a football knee. But these were minor troubles, and on 24th October the motor party started as the advance guard of the Southern Party.

Lieut. Evans was in charge, with Day, Lashly and Hooper. Their object was to take two motor sledges, with three tons of stores, dragging the heavy weight in this way to save the ponies' legs over the hard sea ice. This slippery and hummocky ice was too much for the motors, which worked on the tank principle, with roller chains instead of wheels: these chains slipped and wore on the ice, while the engines over-heated.

Scott watched the progress of this new form of transport with anxiety, Evans and his men had a stiff task. Here and there they made ground satisfactorily, but mainly they had to haul the sledges themselves.

They did reach the Great Barrier, but near Safety Camp Lashly's motor broke down with a big end smashed; Day and Lashly worked all night on repairs with the temperature — 25 degrees.

Eventually they struggled as far as Corner Camp, fifty-one miles over the hummocked ice, and there, much to Day's disappointment, the motor sledges had to be abandoned. At least they had dragged the stores for

29

the Southern Party over a surface which would have tried the ponies very hard, and to that extent they were justified. Scott, proceeding with the ponies, came upon the abandoned machines, and was distressed; but he had not based his calculations upon much help from them, and the march continued.

Their route was clear, straight across the Barrier along the line of the depot-laying journey, up the Beardmore Glacier, and due south for the Pole. Some 900 miles of hard going, but they picked up the cairns laid on the previous year quite easily, and Scott noted that the surface was good, so that the ponies rarely sank to the fetlock joint.

Scott, with Wilson, led one party; Crean, Atkinson, Wright and Keohane looked after the ponies. Lieut. Evans and his party in the meanwhile had gone ahead to Mount Hooper.

For a while all went well. On 9th November Scott recorded beautiful weather, with a temperature of — 12 degrees. Then, unexpectedly, difficulties began.

A very horrid march into a strong head wind and a snowstorm made Scott anxious about the weather conditions. The surface was deplorable —soft crust and drifts of snow; and overhead the sky was black and the atmosphere dark and depressing. The little party trudged on, leading their ponies, hoping against hope for an improvement, approaching One Ton Camp over the great snow plain which stretched away into the darkness.

Oates found that the ponies were losing condition rather more rapidly than he had thought likely—an ominous sign; but they continued to make their fifteen miles a day, though the surface deteriorated as they went along. By 22nd November Scott was rather more cheerful, and seemed to think that they would get through to the Glacier without great difficulty. The weather had improved, and the sun was shining; but gradually the ponies weakened, and on 24th November the first of them, poor old Jehu, had to be shot.

Actually the destruction of the ponies was necessary for other reasons: food was short, and both dogs and men took to horse meat.

Then the wind increased again, and although for two days Scott struggled ahead, on 5th December the party woke up to find a tearing,

30

THE SOUTHERN PARTY.

AN APPROACHING BLIZZARD.

roaring blizzard blowing. With it drove fine, powdered snow, and when Scott went outside he was covered in ice from head to foot in a minute. The ponies, too, were encased in freezing snow, and there were vast drifts above the tents. Even Scott's spirits flagged a little and he wrote in his diary: " What on earth does such weather mean at this time of year? It is more than our share of ill fortune, I think, but the luck may turn yet. . . . No foresight—no procedure—could have prepared us for this state of affairs."

With this most unseasonal weather came high temperatures: it was + 31, and inside the tents everything was soaked—clothes, sleeping-bags, boots—while pools of water lay everywhere. Keohane burst into rhyme about these wretched conditions, saying:

> " *The snow is all melting and everything's afloat.*
> *If this goes on much longer,*
> *We shall have to turn the* tent *upside down,*
> *And use it as a boat.*"

A proof of wonderful good humour in the circumstances.

Still the blizzard went on, and Scott wrote: " Miserable, utterly miserable. We have camped in the ' Slough of Despond.' . . . Oh, but this is too crushing, and we are only twelve miles from the Glacier. A hopeless feeling descends on one and is hard to fight off. What immense patience is needed for such occasions! "

Patience, indeed, and more than that, for Scott became gravely anxious. Weather like this in December was wholly beyond any reasonable calculations, and to be delayed against all expectations for four days, with men and dogs kept on full rations, was a really serious blow to Scott's hopes of success.

It threw his plans out entirely, and although they did manage to move, with great exertion, on 9th December, all the ponies had to be shot at Camp 31, just short of the Barrier. They called the place Shambles Camp.

Despite all their troubles they remained cheerful. The great granite pillars of the Gateway were before them, and they could see the spur of Mount Hope, an encouraging name.

31

The sledges were divided thus:

1. Scott, Wilson, Oates and P. O. Evans.
2. E. Evans, Atkinson, Wright, Lashly.
3. Bowers, Cherry-Garrard, Crean, Keohane.

Leaving Shambles Camp, they made about two miles an hour, but soon they began to rise, and the going was hard; often they sank into the snow almost to their knees, and the sledge went down to the cross-bars.

Scott was worried about Lieut. Evans's party, who had been given the hardest work. For five weeks Evans and Lashly had man-hauled, and they could not be expected to be as fresh as the others, who had led ponies until 18th December.

There was a stiff pull before them, moreover, for they were mounting the steady slope of the Beardmore Glacier—an uphill tug, with danger of crevasses, and 10,000 feet to climb. The Glacier is 120 miles long, a daunting prospect, especially as the lower valley was filled with snow brought by the blizzard; this meant that the party had to plough through often up to the knees, while the sledges frequently stuck. Every time they sank, the effort to drag them out was terrible. The new snow was still soft; the crust beginning to form on it was not yet strong enough to support sledges and men; but for their skis, there would have been a complete hold-up.

A typical day was 13th December, when they started at 8 a.m., and found a crust which would not hold the sledges. The sun shone and it was hot enough to make them sweat until their clothes were soaked; they heaved and strained until camping time at 7 p.m. and then had covered a bare four miles.

Woefully disheartening, Scott called it, and conditions were getting worse instead of better. Some of the party suffered severely from snow blindness. Their lips were raw and blistered. They got so terribly hot pulling that Scott began to fear, if there was trouble on the Summit, it would be " mostly due to the chill falling on sunburned skins." The outlook was depressing, and the weather gloomy.

Gradually they worked their way up the Glacier, sometimes coming

DAY AND LASHLY REPAIRING A MOTOR SLEDGE.

PONIES BENEATH THEIR SNOW-WALL SHELTER.

PITCHING THE TENT.

across thirty-foot ice hollows, down which they would slide on their sledges, hauling them up on the other side with tremendous difficulty. The physical exertion needed on this journey was enormous, and only men of remarkable strength and stamina could have carried on hauling day after day in such exacting conditions.

There was some improvement in the surface as they approached Upper Glacier Depot, where Scott had the unpleasant task of warning the party who were to return—Atkinson, Wright, Cherry-Garrard and Keohane. These four were very disappointed, though they realised that Scott had to make some decision in the matter.

Next crevasses began to trouble them, and they all had severe falls; but by 22nd December the summit of the Glacier was reached and the third stage of the journey began.

On the flyleaf of his notebook Scott recorded the ages of his party—himself 43, Wilson, 39, Petty Officer Evans 37, Oates 32, Bowers 28—average age 36. It is amazing that men no longer young could so withstand the rigours of the expedition.

By this time they were marching fourteen and fifteen miles a day, with a searching wind blowing from the south-south-east; and Lashly celebrated Christmas Day—and his birthday—by falling into a crevasse: an unpleasant experience which did not worry him in the slightest degree. He went down very suddenly and almost took the crew with him. The others had to wait for half an hour while Lashly was hauled out with Alpine rope. He reported that the crevasse was U-shaped, fifty feet deep and eight feet across. Naturally his arrival at the top coincided with a shower of cordial Christmas and birthday wishes!

That evening they had a Christmas supper: a full whack of pemmican, with slices of horse meat flavoured with onion and curry powder and thickened with biscuit: an arrowroot, cocoa and biscuit hoosh, sweetened; a plum pudding; cocoa and raisins, caramels and ginger. And Bowers said to Lieut. Evans: " Teddy, if all is well next Christmas, we'll get hold of all the poor children we can, and just stuff them full of nice things, won't we? "

Scott notes the fact that after this feast—he calls it a tightener—they all slept splendidly and felt warm, which was decidedly unusual.

C

33

They were nearly 10,000 feet up by then, and Scott discovered that the second party had been loading their sledges badly, and had so given themselves unnecessary labour. He told them to find out the cause of the trouble and put it right, but he began to think again that they were tiring, a factor which made him anxious.

The party, for all that, was happy and hopeful. Evans, Crean and Lashly converted the twelve-foot sledges to ten foot, and on 3rd January Scott had the unhappy task of telling these three men that they would have to return. Teddy Evans, says Scott, was terribly disappointed, but took it very well, " and behaved like a man. Poor old Crean wept, and even Lashly was affected "; and indeed it must have been a disappointment to come so far, and then to be sent back when they were almost in sight of the Pole. An exaggeration, perhaps, as the Pole was still 150 miles away, but everything was going smoothly at last, and Scott could only wonder when the luck would turn again.

He was at any rate delighted with his companions: Wilson, unselfish doctor, dexterous cook, tough as steel on the traces, a man of rare spirit and sensibility; Petty Officer Evans, a giant worker with a really remarkable head-piece; little Bowers, indefatigable, oblivious of the cold, organiser extraordinary; Oates, who had been invaluable with the ponies, and now went hard the whole time, as tough and uncomplaining and determined as the rest of them.

Scott was generous in appreciation of his four comrades, but he himself was so clearly the leader, his courage unfailing, his patience unlimited, his judgment never faltering, and all the while he noted the circumstances of their march with the keenest interest. His powers of observation were remarkable—and he was not only the practical man of action. The beauty of natural phenomena never ceased to move him; the roots of his character went deep.

Five extraordinary men, and when they set up their little green tent in that wilderness of snow on 9th January they had passed Shackleton's farthest journey south, and all before them was new country.

They found the monotony of marching heavy upon them, and once more conditions became difficult. They were working on a narrow margin: their supply of food would last them eighteen days: all depended on

"THAT EVENING THEY HAD CHRISTMAS SUPPER."

"IT WAS A BLACK FLAG—THE NORWEGIAN FLAG. AMUNDSEN WAS FIRST AT THE POLE."

their ability to keep their marches long enough. The surface was terrible: the sledge rasped and creaked.

Scott said on 11th January: " I have never had such pulling . . . have covered six miles, but at fearful cost to ourselves . . . about seventy-five miles from the Pole—can we keep this up for seven days? It takes it out of us like anything. None of us ever had such hard work before."

The sun was casting shadows, and steering was difficult; the snow was soft, and their prospects did not seem too promising. They cheered up in the evening when they camped, encouraging one another, drawing on reserves for fresh energies; but then would come the appalling weariness of the next day's hauling, with doubt haunting them, and no certainty that conditions would improve.

For all that, they were advancing. By sheer will power they forced their way on, dragging their sledge through the sand-like surface snow, Scott steering as best he could in an appalling light. And as they approached the Pole their spirits rose. Less than forty miles to go—only twenty-seven miles: " We ought to do it now "—and then a smashing blow.

On 16th January they marched well in the morning, and were exhilarated at the thought that the following day should find them at their journey's end. After the mid-day break they set off happily—when suddenly Bowers saw something ahead, a black speck, unnatural in the waste of snow. Scott hurried on towards it, half fearing what he would find. It was a black flag—the Norwegian flag. Nearby were the remains of a camp; in the snow the marks of many dogs' feet. Amundsen and the Norwegians were first at the Pole.

To men who had endured so much and hoped so greatly the sudden bitter disappointment was terrible. " All the day-dreams must go," said Scott. " It will be a wearisome return." The exhilaration was shaken out of them: they could only talk and talk, conscious of having been forestalled. To-morrow they would reach the Pole, but how different it would be, this great moment in their lives upon which they had already expended so much toil!

They lay in their tent, thinking. Scott was sorry for his companions; Bowers and Wilson, Evans and Oates felt bitterly the disappointment of the situation for their leader. They did not sleep much, and at 7.30 the next day they started.

A bitter head wind met them: the temperature was — 22 degrees. The air was damp and cold. They were chilled to the bone. The wind blew dismally. The sky was overcast. " Great God," wrote Scott. " This is an awful place and terrible enough for us to have laboured to it without the reward of priority. Well, it is something to have got here. . . ."

Something indeed, though it was not till next morning, 18th January, 1912, that their observations convinced them that they were actually a mile beyond the Pole and three miles to the right. They moved in that direction, and found a tent. Inside were the names of five Norwegians —Roald Amundsen, Olav Olavson Bjaaland, Hilmer Hanssen, Sverre H. Hassel, Oscar Wisting. And the date on the record was 16th December, 1911.

They found a note from Amundsen, asking Scott to forward a letter to King Haakon. They examined the miscellaneous gear which the Norwegians had left behind. They fastened the Union Jack to a stick and left it as near the South Pole as they could fix the position. They took photographs of Amundsen's tent and Wilson sketched. Then wearily they turned away, to face the ghastly monotony of the return journey—800 miles of solid dragging—conscious that they had been anticipated.

" Well," wrote Scott, " we have turned our back now on the goal of our ambition . . . and goodbye to most of the day-dreams! "

It was inevitable, this heavy reaction, and an ill preparation for the rigours of the march ahead. Scott knew that everything depended on their keeping up a high average, and they set off on the 150-mile stage to Three Degree Depot.

Still the surface was bad, and the work was desperately hard. Scott noted with considerable uneasiness that Oates and Evans seemed to be feeling the cold more than the rest of the party. On 23rd January a blizzard was blowing, and Evans had frost-bite. Next day the wind had risen to full gale force, and they had great difficulty in putting the tent up, so cold were their fingers.

AT THE POLE.

" BY SHEER WILL-POWER THEY FORCED THEIR WAY ON."

The weather was disquieting. It showed signs of breaking up, and they had the terrible summit journey still before them. Food was short. Oates and Evans were frost-bitten. Wilson's eyes gave him great pain. Only tough little Bowers and Scott himself were untouched. To add to their troubles, their sleeping-bags were wet through and they were slowly growing more hungry.

They were tired men, in short, and the sort of troubles they could have coped with when they were fit hit them with double force. Wilson strained a muscle in his leg, and that was a disaster. Evans lost two nails off his frost-bitten hand, and appeared to lose heart. In normal times they could have faced relatively minor accidents like these cheerfully; and, as it was, we can find no traces of bitterness in the diaries they left behind them. There was only that shrugging of the shoulders, that underlying suggestion of acquiescence and resignation with which even brave men, when they are weary mentally and physically, may accept misfortune as inevitable.

They put in a couple of good marches, but their luck did not hold long. Scott fell and hurt his shoulder on a steep slope, and two days later he and Evans fell into a crevasse, a fall which gave Evans unsuspected concussion.

The strain of these forced marches was tremendous. The party grew steadily hungrier. They needed terrific energy to fight on day after day, hauling their sledge over the great ice hummocks, manoeuvring among open crevasses, battered all the while by winds, bitterly cold winds, which slashed their faces to ribbons. Evans's cuts and wounds were suppurating; his nose was badly frost-bitten. Scott was exceedingly anxious about him.

More than anything else, perhaps, Scott felt the responsibility for the safety of the Expedition. He had worked out his plans with the utmost care, but the weather had constantly frustrated him, and already he suspected that they might not come through.

They had managed to keep nearly to schedule in their dreadful journey across the Summit, but injuries had thrown heavier loads on those who remained fit; Evans was a passenger, and seemed to be going steadily downhill.

To the detached observer, the Summit journey was a triumph of will-power and determination: to Scott and his men it had been a nightmare, and when they turned in wearily at night, dazed by effort and incessant cold, weary beyond measure, there was always the prospect of hundreds of miles of this desperate struggle ahead of them. Their sleeping-bags were wet; they did not rest well enough. Food was short and their last day on the Summit, 9th February, found them toiling across a maze of crevasses and sastrugi—the great waves of frozen snow thrown up by the wind.

They had crossed the Summit, though, and Scott hoped for better conditions; but when they reached Mount Darwin they were horrified to find themselves a biscuit-box short—a full day's allowance—and neither Bowers nor Scott could account for this serious mishap.

By then their journey in the Summit camps was done and the party set off more hopefully on the next stage of the journey—down the Beardmore Glacier—encouraged by the thought that warmer conditions might help the unfortunate Evans.

This was a terrible time. Crevasses and steep ice slopes, landfalls and icefalls, made every moment tense with strain and physical effort. The descent of the Glacier took only one day less than the ascent, and its toll of the nerves and energies of the little group of men was a heavy one.

At first the wind was still strong and cold, but when they had advanced some way into the moraine they found conditions so interesting that Scott decided to camp for the day and spend the time in geological research, a decision which showed the remarkable quality of these men, who could detach themselves from their troubles so swiftly that they followed Wilson's investigations with the utmost enthusiasm.

Wilson discovered coal seams in the Beacon sandstone, bearing plant impressions here and there. The whole party felt immensely relieved to be out of the everlasting wind and in a warmer temperature. Scott said it was like going ashore after a sea voyage, and his hopes soared again. They would pull through, he wrote. They were by no means worn out.

It was strange how hope and despair alternated on this journey. No sooner were their spirits mounting with the changed circumstances than the sun disappeared, a northerly wind blew the snow in their faces, and it was impossible to steer. Sunday, 11th February, was "the worst day we have had during the trip and greatly owing to our own fault."

The light was very bad, giving queer shapes and outlines to the ice hummocks and throwing bewildering shadows. Unhappily they turned east, plunging for six hours out of their course, and ending up in the most difficult ice conditions Scott had ever experienced. They lost direction, and found themselves in a maze of crevasses where it was impossible to use skis. For hours they stumbled and plunged on foot on the hard, treacherous ice, slipping, falling constantly into crevasses, desperate with anxiety. Scott's resolution held them together, and they did not give up; but it was 10 p.m. before they fought their way back to the right track, after twelve hours of blind, staggering endeavour, obsessed by anxiety, afraid that they were lost and trapped in that desolation of broken, menacing ice.

To add to their troubles, food was running short. They had three pemmican meals left, and could only hope that they were headed for the next depot. They could last, perhaps, for a day and a half, but the situation was exceedingly critical.

Next day their perplexities increased. The morning went well, but in the afternoon by some mischance they kept too far to the left; once more they were trapped in a terrible confusion of broken ice, crevasses and fissures, a surface which made their progress perilous indeed. They could not agree upon the best direction to take: their course was erratic; they were altogether uncertain of the depot; and they had to reach it next day without fail, for only one meal remained in their bag.

A tight corner, indeed, but with an effort, as Scott notes, they were cheerful, which meant that he set himself to reviving the spirits of his despondent party, though his own doubts and anxieties were grave. Now and again during the night he went outside the tent and saw, much to his alarm, that the sky was overcast, and snow was beginning to fall. In the morning conditions were serious; they could see nothing; all they could do was to remain in their sleeping-bags, wondering what lay before them.

At 9 o'clock they had tea and one biscuit, reserving the little

39

remaining pemmican for the last emergency; soon afterwards they started off, winding through the crevasses.

By great good fortune they stumbled upon an old moraine track. Gradually the way became smoother. Suddenly Evans shouted: "Depot ahead." It was only an ice shadow, and still they plodded on. At last Wilson noticed something—looked again—was certain it was the depot flag—they were saved.

Here they found three and a half days' food, and a meal put new heart into them, though Scott determined that never again must they run so short of provisions. The insecurity of the last ten days had shaken them. Bowers and Wilson were suffering horribly from snow-blindness. Evans could give no help, and was evidently sinking.

There were, indeed, signs that the incessant strain was beginning to tell on the whole party. Scott wrote the next evening, 14th February: "There is no getting away from the fact that we are not pulling strong. Probably none of us: Wilson's leg still troubles him and he doesn't like to trust himself on ski; but the worst case is Evans, who is giving us serious anxiety. This morning he suddenly disclosed a huge blister on his foot. It delayed us on the march, when he had to have his crampons readjusted. Sometimes I fear he is going from bad to worse, but I trust he will pick up again when we come to steady work on ski like this afternoon. He is hungry and so is Wilson. We can't risk opening out our food again, and as cook at present I am serving something under full allowance. We are inclined to get slack and slow with our camping arrangements, and small delays increase. I have talked of the matter to-night and hope for improvement. We cannot do distance without the hours."

That is a significant entry. For the first time Scott admits their signs of waning strength. The men were flagging: for weeks they had endured incredible hardships, but even their amazing fortitude was failing them. Scott was anxious, and quick to detect the slightest falling off in the high standards he set; but he realised better than anyone else the small margin which lay between success and failure. If they kept indomitably to their schedule, and fought against the weariness of body and mind which was insidiously creeping upon them, they would pull through. If for a day they relaxed even a little, they would meet disaster.

Evans's state of health worried them all. He could do nothing to help the work of the journey, and the pyschological effect of his weakening was inevitably depressing. The amazing thing is that he kept going so long; but on 16th February Scott said: " Evans has nearly broken down in brain, we think . . . Perhaps all will be well if we can get to our depot to-morrow fairly early, but it is anxious work with the sick man."

Evans slept well that night, and said, as he always did, that he was quite fit. Next morning he started as usual in the traces, but had to fall out soon with his ski shoes adrift.

The day was gloomy, overcast and misty; soft snow clogged the sledge runners and the little party moved like ghosts through the shadows. The sledge groaned behind them, and before long they had to wait for Evans, who came up very slowly. Again he fell out, and Scott told him not to be long adjusting his shoes. He seemed to be cheerful as he answered. The sledge party had to move on, for the going was stiff; they laboured towards the Monument Rock, where Scott stopped for lunch, since Evans was a long way behind. For a while they did not worry about him; but when they had eaten their meal and he still did not appear, they all started back on ski.

Scott reached him first, and was horrified to find him on his knees, with his hands uncovered and frost-bitten. It was terrible to see this immensely powerful man, whose physical strength and practical ability had been invaluable on the outward journey, reduced to such pitiable weakness and collapse. He said, speaking slowly and with effort, that he did not know what had happened to him. He thought he must have fainted.

Scott tried to get him to his feet, but he sank down again at every other step. Wilson, Bowers and Scott went for the sledge, and put Evans upon it. He was quite comatose when they reached the tent, and at 12.30 a.m. he died quietly. Wilson was certain that he had injured his brain in a fall.

They talked for a while, and then moved on over the pressure ridges down to Lower Glacier Depot. A terrible night, but the death of Evans

41

did relieve them of the handicap of a sick companion, and on Sunday, 18th February, fortified by a big meal of horse meat, they started out on their last march across the Ross Barrier surface.

Scott was apprehensive, and with reason, for the surface was even worse than he had expected—hard, with a covering of loose snow, which checked the sledge, giving it no glide, and making them feel that they might as well be pulling over desert sand.

For three days the going was desperately hard, and they knew that they were racing for time. The season was advancing rapidly, and they could not afford to waste an hour. Fortunately these extraordinary men refused to be downcast. Scott commented upon the determined cheerfulness of Wilson and Bowers, and he himself continued to lead with all his old resolution and outward confidence. Beyond doubt, however, their situation was critical, and Scott watched the length of their marches with anxious care.

They made the miles, but the labour was immense, and they were tired.

On 23rd February they picked up the regular line of cairns, which encouraged them, but they found a shortage of oil in the depots, due to perishing of the leather stoppers in the great cold, and unexpected evaporation and leakage. This was a blow, for it meant that they had to be extremely careful with their fuel for cooking.

Actually for a while the weather was fine; but they needed a wind to help them, and the irregular and clinging surface constantly hampered them. The temperature at night was dropping tremendously—on 26th February the thermometer went to — 40 degrees, and Scott wrote: " Things must be critical until we reach the depot, and the more I think of matters, the more I anticipate their remaining so after that event. . . . There is no doubt the middle of the Barrier is a pretty awful locality."

Awful it must have been, with the cold so intense that it took them an hour and a half to put their foot gear on before they started in the morning. Still the dragging was back-breaking, and when on 2nd March they staggered into the Middle Barrier depot, three misfortunes overtook them.

Oates showed his toes very badly frost-bitten: the oil again was very short—scarcely enough, even with the greatest economy, to carry them to their next depot: the wind brought heavily overcast weather, and next day they lost cairns and tracks and could only make five and a half miles on a surface which was worse than ever.

They knew then beyond doubt that their position was critical. " Amongst ourselves," said Scott, " we are unendingly cheerful, but what each man feels in his heart I can only guess." The surface was coated with a thin layer of woolly crystal, which caused friction on the runners of the sledge, and made it almost immovable. Next day they covered only four and a half miles, and the prospect was grim.

Their courage and determination never faltered. Still to one another they kept up the pretence of optimism, though as they heaved at the sledge they must have known how frail were their chances, and as the sledge stuck time after time their weary bodies must have wilted, and their minds grown dazed.

The scene is clear enough. The vast waste of the Barrier surface, whipped into ice waves by the bitter winds; the four men bowed in their harness, straining at the ropes, their small sledge creaking behind them: four men in that frozen wilderness, encircled by the blue Polar shadows, fighting onwards, creeping ahead day by day, lying by night in that green tent, flayed by cold, suffering, yet talking casually about their future plans.

In their hearts they knew what lay ahead, but nothing could break their spirit. The fuel was alarmingly low, and Bowers, Wilson and Scott watched Oates with the greatest misgivings. Oates was very lame: his feet had swollen. Wilson doctored him with wonderful solicitude, and suffered horribly from the cold himself in consequence.

The low temperatures had taken them by surprise, and it was all the more unfortunate that the fuel was running out. They could have little hot food: they ate pemmican solid, with only the chill off, and pretended they preferred it that way.

Oates was holding them back fatally. They all realised that the drag of an unfit man meant the difference between safety and disaster, but not one of them complained.

Oates himself was wonderfully stoical: his feet must have been terribly painful: he sat wretchedly on the sledge when the shocking visibility made his companions unharness themselves to search for the track: he forced himself to be cheerful. The only signs they had of his suffering were his long silences in the tent. They did all they could to help and encourage him, and they still talked of what they would do together at home.

Never did men make a more gallant fight against cruelly adverse circumstances. Their rate of advance was approximately a mile an hour, harder work than any they had endured, with less result. They wondered whether the dogs had been to Mount Hooper. That would give them a chance. They discussed the prospect of an oil shortage at the next depot.

Wilson's feet gave trouble next, mainly because, in his unselfish care for others, he neglected his own safety. The time they spent each morning getting into their gear worried Scott increasingly.

By 8th March they realised that Oates could not hope to get through. His left foot had gone irretrievably, but his pluck remained. He asked Wilson on 10th March if he had a chance and Wilson could only be non-committal, though he realised that none of them had more than the barest chance at all.

They reached Mount Hooper Depot, but the dogs had not been there. Actually for six days they had been waiting at One Ton Depot with Cherry-Garrard, eighty miles further on. Cherry-Garrard had been held up by blizzards, and was short of food. He had to choose between pushing forward one more march, with barely enough rations to bring the dogs back, and the great risk of missing Scott, or waiting at One Ton Depot, where Scott was bound to call if he managed to pull through. Cherry-Garrard decided to wait. It was the only decision in the circumstances forced upon him by weather which continually seemed to conspire against the Expedition.

In the meanwhile Scott and his men faced the situation with their customary fortitude. There was a shortage of provisions and fuel at Mount Hooper. The weather was breaking and a wind from the west-north-west made them settle down in a comfortless camp. There Oates calmly discussed his position.

" THE GREAT WAVES OF FROZEN SNOW THROWN UP BY THE WIND."

TENT ON THE BEARDMORE GLACIER.

" He is a brave fine fellow," said Scott, " and understands the situation, but he practically asked for advice." They did the only thing possible to men of such character, urging Oates to march with them as long as he could, realising that his presence reduced to nothing their own slender chances of survival.

After they had talked, Scott made Wilson take opium tabloids from the medicine chest and hand them round, so that they should have the means of ending their agonies if they decided to do so. It was the easy way out, with death apparently inevitable, but they did not take it.

They struggled on. The sky was overcast, and they were stumbling into darkness, with seven days' food, fifty-five miles to cover to One Ton Camp, and some six miles a day all they could manage. Calmly Scott worked out the figures and noted them down, with the inevitable conclusion that even at the best they would be thirteen miles short of safety when food gave out.

Poor Oates was still trying to do his share of work, pushing feebly with hands almost as bad as his feet. The cold was intense, beyond all expectations. On 14th March they woke to find a strong northerly wind blowing, and the temperature — 37 degrees. That day they could only march five miles before the bitter air became unendurable, and with difficulty they made camp. " Truly awful outside the tent," said Scott; " must fight it out to the last biscuit, but can't reduce rations."

Then came a tragic day, probably Saturday, 17th, though Scott confessed that he had lost track of dates. Oates had come to the end of his tether, with no strength left and suffering incredible pain. He asked to be left behind in his sleeping-bag, but they persuaded him to make the afternoon march, and he stuck it out uncomplaining. He was worse that night, and his companions knew that he could go on no longer. He went to sleep, not expecting to wake, but in the morning he woke again. There was a blizzard blowing. Conditions were terrible. Scott, Wilson and Bowers watched Oates as he struggled painfully to his feet. He said, " I am just going outside, and may be some time." His companions tried to dissuade him. They knew what his action meant. He shook his head, opened the flap of the tent, and walked out into the blizzard. They did not see him again.

45

Scott's own comment on this is sufficient. "It was the act," he said, " of a brave man and an English gentleman. We all hope to meet the end with a similar spirit, and assuredly the end is not far."

Even then they refused to give in. They were cold on the march, and small wonder, for at mid-day the temperature was — 40 degrees. Scott's companions were unendingly cheerful, and talked with him of getting through. He played up to them; never has there been nobler acting, more dogged courage. That they could survive at all, worn out and racked with pain, was amazing; that they could still go forward into that terrible wind and make light of their troubles was the highest heroism. The pity of it was that they had come so near to safety—twenty miles. Two long marches from One Ton Depot, that was all.

The next morning, 18th March, they faced a head wind from the north-west and it stopped them for a while; no human being could have faced it. Scott, still keeping his diary, chided himself for mixing a small spoonful of curry powder in his melted pemmican. It kept him awake and in pain all night: the next day he felt ill on the march, and his right foot went. He did not complain—just recorded the fact as an instance of carelessness. More significant was the realisation that they had reached the last half fill of oil in their primus—that and a little spirit stood between them and thirst.

Even so they were not finished. The wind went round and was fair; it might help them. They camped with difficulty on 19th March, and unexpectedly found that their food warmed them, and enabled them to sleep well. They stumbled along, bowed and straining at a sledge which seemed strangely heavy, three weary figures in a desolate landscape: the wind was in their faces again, blowing bitterly out of the north, giving them no chance. They camped at last within eleven miles of One Ton Depot, where food and fuel awaited them.

That Monday night they turned into their sleeping-bags with still a faint, persistent glimmer of hope. Only eleven miles to go—it seemed so little when they had endured so long. They talked and went to sleep. When they woke a severe blizzard was raging outside their little tent.

That was the last cruel blow. All Tuesday they lay in their bags, waiting for the weather to change. On Wednesday conditions were no

46

THE RESTING-PLACE OF SCOTT AND HIS COMPANIONS.

HOMEWARD BOUND.

better, and they decided upon a forlorn hope. Wilson and Bowers would go to the depot for fuel; still they refused to be beaten.

Wilson and Bowers could not start. The blizzard continued, roaring round the tent. They made their last decision. They would die naturally; they would march for the depot, the three of them together, march until they fell. Even that they were denied. For nine days the gale raged on; every day they were ready to start their last journey, but always the flailing snowstorm held them fast.

On 20th March they had enough fuel to make two cups of tea apiece, and food for two more days. On 29th March Scott made the last entry in his diary. " I do not think we can hope for any better things now," he wrote; " we shall stick it out to the end, but we are getting weaker, of course, and the end cannot be far. It seems a pity, but I do not think I can write any more. R. Scott." Then, a final note: " For God's sake look after our people."

Eight months later a search party found the tent, with snow drifted high around it. Inside were the three bodies. Wilson and Bowers lay with their sleeping-bags closed over their heads. Scott apparently was the last to die. He lay between them, with his coat open, the flaps of his sleeping-bag thrown back, his arm across Wilson. The temperature was — 20 degrees then, and the Barrier wind blew bitterly: but the men who found them stood bareheaded by the tent.

# BRITISH ANTARCTIC EXPEDITION
## 1910

### OFFICERS

| | |
|---|---|
| Robert Falcon Scott | Captain, C.V.O., R.N. |
| Edward R. G. R. Evans | Lieutenant, R.N. |
| Victor L. A. Campbell | Lieutenant, R.N. (Emergency List). |
| Henry R. Bowers | Lieutenant, R.I.M. |
| Lawrence E. G. Oates | Captain, 6th Inniskilling Dragoons. |
| G. Murray Levick | Surgeon, R.N. |
| Edward L. Atkinson | Surgeon, R.N., Parasitologist. |

### SCIENTIFIC STAFF

| | |
|---|---|
| Edward Adrian Wilson | B.A., M.B.(Cantab.), Chief of the Scientific Staff, and Zoologist. |
| George C. Simpson | D.Sc., Meteorologist. |
| T. Griffith Taylor | B.A., B.Sc., B.E., Geologist. |
| Edward W. Nelson | Biologist. |
| Frank Debenham | B.A., B.Sc., Geologist. |
| Charles S. Wright | B.A., Physicist. |
| Raymond E. Priestley | Geologist. |
| Herbert G. Ponting | F.R.G.S., Camera Artist. |
| Cecil H. Meares | In Charge of Dogs. |
| Bernard C. Day | Motor Engineer. |
| Apsley Cherry-Garrard | B.A., Assistant Zoologist. |
| Tryggve Gran | Sub-Lieutenant, Norwegian N.R., B.A., Ski Expert. |

### MEN

| | |
|---|---|
| W. Lashly | Chief Stoker, R.N. |
| W. W. Archer | Chief Steward, late R.N. |
| Thomas Clissold | Cook, late R.N. |
| Edgar Evans | Petty Officer, R.N. |
| Robert Forde | Petty Officer, R.N. |
| Thomas Crean | Petty Officer, R.N. |
| Thomas S. Williamson | Petty Officer, R.N. |
| Patrick Keohane | Petty Officer, R.N. |
| George P. Abbott | Petty Officer, R.N. |
| Frank V. Browning | Petty Officer, 2nd Class, R.N. |
| Harry Dickason | Able Seaman, R.N. |
| F. J. Hooper | Steward, late R.N. |
| Anton Omelchenko | Groom. |
| Demetri Gerof | Dog Driver. |